ANONYMOUS METHOD

BY

Zahid Fayyaz
Artworks By: Leena Kewlani

About the author

Zahid grew up in the inner city, Bristol. His childhood was filled with playing a lot of sports- cricket, football, squash and karting, until it was time to go study and 'make something of himself'. He wanted to be a F1 race engineer, so he went to study Mechanical Engineering. After a year, he realised that it wasn't for him. It wasn't creative enough. He was always the class clown and loved playing in front of people. Engineering was missing the interaction with people that he lived for. He has always been fascinated by people. He was always imitating people, telling stories, people watching and trying to understand the world around him and what made people do what they do. He then stumbled upon acting classes and that changed his life for good. It allowed him to analyse characters and embody them. He worked hard for two years and got himself a place at the prestigious Lee Strasberg Institute in New York city, studying Acting & creative writing. The method helped him understand himself, life and the world around him to an even deeper level. As he started to understand himself more, he was able find common ground and 'lend parts of himself to the characters.' He developed an eye for detail and became more observant of the world around him. Observing the world helped him develop as a writer and those extra details to characters, to really bring them to life. Having graduated, he was set on becoming an actor (and still is, but it's kinda on the back burner for now) but he'd get call after call for shows that would depict himself in a bad light. The stereotypical roles such as 'the terrorist', cab driver, or villager 7 in a big movie just so the studio can meet their diversity quota. Being a jobbing actor and scriptwriter, he needed something to do to keep his memory fresh off all that he had learned. So, he started to type up his notes from Strasberg, to Tumblr (when that was a thing). Eventually he ran out of notes to publish, so he started to write his own thoughts, observations and poems. It started to gain traction and grew bigger and bigger. Then Instagram took over, so he moved over and during the pandemic, the numbers quickly shot up gaining retweets from actors and public figures from around the world. He then gave up his anonymity and started to interact and go live with his followers. It was his followers who suggested he compile a book with his works. It was their encouragement, which gave him the confidence to get back to script writing again. And in the past year, he has just completed his first full length play. We hope you all enjoy the book and share it with your loved ones. Maybe if all goes well, there might be a part two…

Buying The Artworks

The artworks have been created by Leena Kewlani, and can be bought on www.artezaar.com or you can email her on Leena@artezaar.com to purchase it directly.

Each painting – you can either buy the original artwork or you can buy a print.

Leena will be donating the profits of the sale of the artworks towards supporting a Special Needs school.

How Leena's Artworks became part of Anonymous Method's journey...

They say everything is destined. I stumbled upon Anonymous Method's account randomly on Instagram, and once we connected, it felt like I found an old friend. I loved how his quotes/poems/notes provoked me, brought out emotions and got me thinking. Especially since we connected during the pandemic, when so many people around us were dealing with loneliness. We all understood the deadly impact of the pandemic, but yet, we wanted it all to disappear (which of course it didn't!).

What got me through the pandemic and lockdowns was art. I expanded and grew my online art gallery business, I painted a lot, and I taught art to kids online. Seeing those little ones every day on Zoom brought so much happiness in my life. For a lot of those kids, we teachers were their only humans outside of their families that they spoke and connected to, and we were blessed to create magic every day.

When we decided to collaborate for this book, I wanted every artwork of mine to reflect the emotion/feeling/thought that Zahid was trying to bring through his notes. Each artwork has been painted on canvas, and I have created a style just for this book. It's very different from my usual bold colours and palette knife strokes. But I sincerely hope my art helps you connect to the book at a deeper level, making you feel more positive about life and everything around us. I have always wanted my paintings to spread joy and positivity in every heart and in every home, and with this book, I am so grateful that my artworks will join hands with Zahid's notes in helping to create that chain of positivity and love.

About Leena Kewlani

Leena Kewlani is a Dubai based Artist, who loves her art to channel positivity and good vibes. Leena worked for 22 years in media and advertising. She was the Regional Communications Director & Head of Content,
Entertainment and Sports Sponsorships, Integrations and Activations (Middle East & North Africa) at Wavemaker, and then she headed up Digital Branded Content at Choueiri Group. She led strategy and execution across multinational accounts, and created award winning content campaigns across various brands.

In 2019, she left the industry to create Artezaar.com Online Art Gallery with her friend, driven by a simple mission: they wanted to help UAE based artists sell their paintings and handicrafts to art buyers and collectors, locally and globally. Today, Artezaar.com features close to 150+ artists with over 1500+ paintings and accessories.

Leena is also a TEDx Speaker, and has exhibited her paintings at Carrousel du Louvre in Paris, Moscow State Museum (Burganov House), World Art in India and UAE, along with other exhibitions in the UAE.

She loves to teach kids art and pottery, helping them express their emotions and grow with confidence. Her dream: to build an art school for kids, where they get opportunities to grow under famous artists.

"I fall in love with imperfections in people, in nature and in things around me. Those imperfections, those little hidden away pieces, and those crazy thoughts that we all have – they all hold a beautiful story. Imperfections are real, they are full of soul. Love and beauty are embedded in imperfection if you choose to see it. I choose to see it." - Leena

More about me on Instagram @leenakewlani.art @artezaar

Introduction

We live in the age of the internet, where we spend most of our time socialising and connecting with people via social media rather than in person. Today we are so connected yet so lonely. We need instant gratification. We need instant results, and if something doesn't work, we just replace it, be it people or things. This has left so many people broken, with no real person to talk to face to face, which is what we need when we are down. I've compiled a collection of thoughts/poems/notes, I don't even know what to call them, but just to make it easier, I'll call them thoughts. I've tried to observe and listen to people over the short time I've been on this planet. I've tried to understand, not judge when listening and observing.

Some have come from life experiences, some from the inner monologues of characters that I have worked on as an actor and others have come from characters that I have written as a scriptwriter. I hope that when you read the excerpts, you connect with them. I hope they help you understand life a bit better. I hope to show you an alternative angle to life's problems. Although I should say one thing, a bit of a disclaimer; my notes aren't applicable to everyone and every single situation. The danger with reading is that sometimes we read something and force the meaning upon our circumstances. You may agree with some and not with others, and that's ok. Some parts won't make sense, that's also ok. If you read this book and enjoy it, I would love for you to share it with friends and family. Let's start a chain of positivity and try make the world a better place.

Real people rarely have friends. They make you see the world and your life for what it is. No facade. And this sends most people running without an explanation.

@anonymousmethod

The biggest cause for low self-esteem today, is the fact that we go around dropping people, just like that. From talking daily, to becoming complete strangers at the drop of a hat. And we don't even bat an eyelid, as if nothings happened. We fail to see the person at the receiving end, who is left with a broken heart & shattered self-esteem.

@anonymousmethod

Sometimes things break your heart, but fix your vision.

@anonymousmethod

No one knows the violence, heartbreak and loneliness it took to become this gentle.

@anonymousmethod

It's heartbreaking when you have to be heartless in a world that doesn't appreciate kindness. Being heartless isn't you, so you just have to let go…

@anonymousmethod

The reason you fuck up a good thing is that you dig too much. No one is perfect, so stop looking for it. Yes, everyone has a past. We all have a history. Work on your future & how you can grow together.

@anonymousmethod

A heart doesn't turn cold, unless it has been treated with a cold shoulder for a while. Fear the day when a good heart gives up on you.

@anonymousmethod

If you truly know what it feels like to have no one help you, then you won't turn a blind eye to someone suffering, someone going through a tough time, someone in pain. Reach out to people & be there for them.

@anonymousmethod

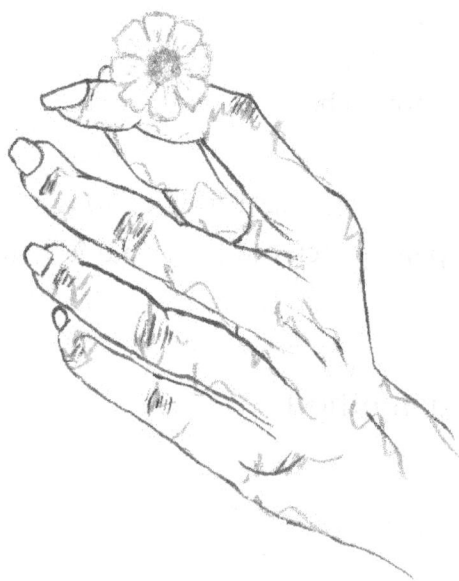

They listen to you cry because they know how it feels to have no one. They encourage you to chase your dreams because they know what it feels like having no one believe in them. They give you gifts because they know what it feels like not having someone give & they trust you because they know the importance of trust when building someone back up. After all this, if you still are unsure about them because they have imperfections, then your judgement is fogged by your past. No one is perfect, but all of the above speaks volumes & should trump the 'imperfections'.

@anonymousmethod

I hadn't felt a connection like this in years. I was always scared of being abandoned, like I had been in the past, from the people that were meant to love me the most. I remember, bravely asking "When will I see you again?". In that moment, behind those words, I sensed a great cry; "Why have people always abandoned me in the past? Why am I the last one out of all my friends to find someone?" Maybe it's because I feel like you're about to abandon me. "Are you going to abandon me?" But the look in her eyes, as we parted ways told me everything I needed to know. And into the distance she disappeared and once again, we became strangers.

@anonymousmethod

It's so easy to end things. Sometimes even before they begin, but before you do, think about the first time you met & how they made you smile. Remember when you used to speak all day, everyday. Even till the early hours of the morning because you enjoyed talking to them more than sleeping. Remember the times you wiped one another's tears & were there for each other when things got bad. Did that make you smile? Now are you sure you want to be strangers for the rest of your lives?

@anonymousmethod

Form your tribe around vision & values. Not any old, outdated social construct.

@anonymousmethod

Don't be afraid to initiate conversation after a conflict. Listen, be heard & heal whatever has taken place between the two of you. Unfinished business stays with you forever. Do it before it's too late.

@anonymousmethod

If you're looking for 'perfect' or your 'true soulmate' then you will be looking till your last breath. 'Perfect' doesn't exist & soulmates don't just appear out of nowhere, they are made through effort & sacrifices.

@anonymousmethod

Never become that person who says, "Let me not care so much" or "Ok, let me show them less love". Never let anyone or any bad experience make you feel this way. Always love hard. Care hard. Nurture hard. Because that's the way you're meant to be. Remember, caring isn't a negative thing.

@anonymousmethod

It was hard for me to open up, because every time I do, people just feel pity for me and most people don't want to hear it. I've learned to just focus on the positives, which made me come across as 'too happy' or 'perfect'. I'm far from it but I choose to focus on being positive rather than dwell on my past, but for some reason this bores people, as I don't entertain drama or 'excitement'. I guess it bored you too. I don't know where I'm going wrong but I just want to be loved for the positive person I have become because of my journey.

@anonymousmethod

You didn't love them. Admit it, you just didn't want to be alone, or maybe they were good for your ego. Or maybe they made you feel better about your miserable life, but you didn't love them. Because you don't destroy the people you love.

@anonymousmethod

No, you didn't lose your self respect by pursuing someone you thought was genuine. In fact, you did the right thing. People use a mask as a survival mechanism. As a way to protect themselves from the hurt that they have endured. Be the person who makes them want to trust again. And even if they don't trust you, then it just goes to show how you're an incredibly genuine person. Just pray for them that one day, they heal from their past. That they overcome this & start trusting once again.

@anonymousmethod

Value them before they are taken away from you &
become a distant memory… yet again.

@anonymousmethod

We are scared to move on because it means we accept our fate of being strangers again. And we'd rather be heartbroken than forget about one another.

@anonymousmethod

3,564 days it took for me to get over my past. I spent years feeling unsafe about opening up to people, because every time I did, I always got short changed. So, I just used humour, sarcasm and a fake smile to hide my scars and not feel anything. It took a million interactions, a thousand books, hours of overthinking and hyping myself up, to feel safe enough to open up again. To be vulnerable. Then I met you, you made me feel so safe that I started believing in people again. I acted like that shit was easy, but it was the bravest thing I've ever done. Only for you to turn around and say, "It wasn't a thing…"

@anonymousmethod

Some people are so used to inconsistency, instability and drama, that when you give them stability and calmness in their lives, they find it boring. They aren't familiar with a life that doesn't contain surprises, be it bad ones, so a steady environment unsettles them.

@anonymousmethod

No one can read your mind. If you want people to know how you feel, tell them. Their lack of awareness isn't always down to their lack of care, sometimes it's down to your lack of communication.

@anonymousmethod

We hurt people but we justify it in our heads by lying to ourselves. All it takes is a simple apology to fix things. Remove your ego & help people rather than leave them worse than you found them.

@anonymousmethod

Not everyone is replaceable. Not everyone is gonna hurt you. Everyone is just trying to keep it together, so stop expecting perfection, it doesn't exist. Don't let this clout chasing, judgmental, emotionally unavailable generation convince you that you should throw people away just like that. Learn to communicate and fix problems before you start to lose valuable people.

@anonymousmethod

If you're uncomfortable, lonely, beaten down, been left for dead and feeling lost, life is telling you to change; so you can grow into the person you are meant to be.

@anonymousmethod

It goes well, almost too well. Green flag after green flag. Then along comes a voice, whispering; "How can this possibly happen to me? Do I deserve this?" And then our mind starts playing tricks on us and all you see are red flags. Stop right there & correct this pattern before you destroy something beautiful... yet again.

@anonymousmethod

You scare away anyone that tries to love you because you were bought up in a home that emotionally neglected you. So, true love feels foreign. Instead, you go for people that are emotionally unavailable, so you can cater to them. Also, there's a lot less to lose because you invest less of your emotions. That's the love you understand. Trust once again, not everyone is out to break you.

@anonymousmethod

If no one wants to die alone, then why do we go around being mean to one another? Sometimes I pretend to be a shitty person, just to fit into todays society. Because every time I'm real, people assume I'm boasting, being pretentious or the classic; too good to be true.

@anonymousmethod

The modern day 'one who got away' is only a click away. You'll be able to see how great they became. You'll see them with their partner and see how perfect they are together. How they became such an amazing parent. You'll see how beautiful their life is; and knowing that could've been you will kill you inside. You'll think where did I go wrong? Well, you overlooked them. You were so quick to judge them & you disposed of them. You called them a 'Simp' for caring. You found their kindness, empathy, vulnerability & honesty as a weakness. You went for what was deemed 'cool' by society- Someone who played hard to get, a 'bad' boy/girl, one who was 'mysterious', one who kept you 'keen'. You realised too late that you can't live with someone like that till 'death did you apart'. It's too late in the day and now 'the one' is just a distant memory. And now you just sit there thinking "If only…"

@anonymousmethod

Please don't ever think I need you in my life. Because at one point, we didn't know one another & I was doing just fine. I'll go back to that.

@anonymousmethod

Problem with being an empath is that you attract broken people. They come into your life, attracted to your kindness, love and empathy. Then one day, they get bored & just leave never to return.

@anonymousmethod

Money helps dress your wounds.

@anonymousmethod

We are a generation obsessed with results but not the work. We love the 'idea' of being 'someone' far more than the actual necessary day to day things that we need to do to become that someone.

@anonymousmethod

Date an artist. How else are you going to become a song, movie, painting, play or a book?

@anonymousmethod

Who did you call when you were in pain? Who did you share the most intimate details of your life? Who did you share your biggest dreams & ambitions? Who did you make up little jokes with, that only the two of you understood? Who did you open your heart up to? If they listened to you, understood you, comforted you & cared about all these things, then they were the one.

@anonymousmethod

We see ourselves through the eyes of people around us. So, remember this; don't take advice from 'unqualified' people who have no peace, as their behaviour has more to do with their internal struggle & lack of peace than it ever did with you.

@anonymousmethod

We can't make people change. They must have a desire inside them to want to change. Communicate with them, give them love, support & show them kindness, but don't hang around waiting, if their desire to change isn't there. Let them be. Let them dwell, they'll soon realise, or maybe they won't, but don't lose yourself whilst trying to help people who don't want to be helped.

@anonymousmethod

Unless you heal yourself, you'll be toxic to anyone that tries to love you.

@anonymousmethod

Rejection teaches you perseverance & how to get tough. It also teaches you that not every path is right for you. You are on a path that is made for you. Sometimes the universe is protecting you from a bad job, a bad experience or a toxic person. So, next time, remember this; when you fail at something or someone leaves you heartbroken; Let yourself be sad, grieve for what didn't happened. It's totally normal to do so. But at the end of it all, please move on. Better things are waiting for you.

@anonymousmethod

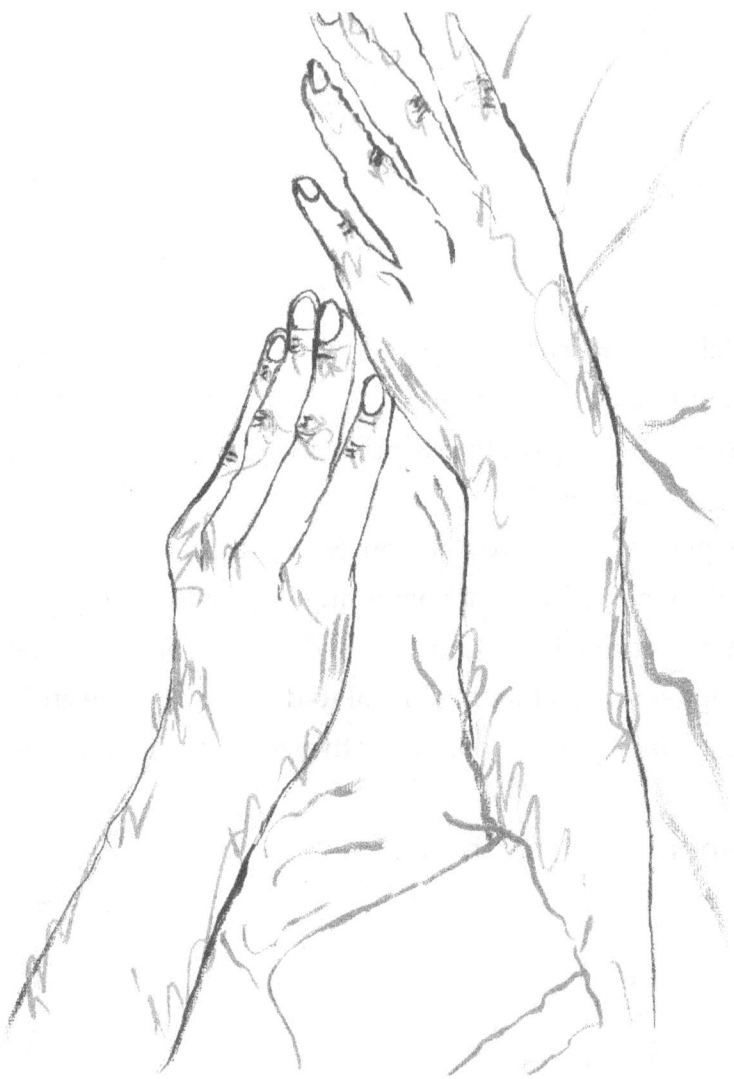

Dear Me, I am so sorry that it's taken me this long to realise & apologise. I am sorry that you gave so much time to fixing people, whilst you were crumbling. I am sorry that I let you put everyone else's healing before yours. I am sorry you had to tell your loved one's white lies, so they didn't find out what was actually going on inside your head. I am sorry about the days your heart was aching, but you still smiled & laughed so no one had to worry about you. I am sorry you gave all your time & love to people who didn't reciprocate. I am sorry that you listened to everyone, whilst there was no one around to listen to you. I am sorry I didn't love you, especially when no one else did. That's the least I could've done.

@anonymousmethod

We put so much time & effort into trying to look 'successful' & 'happy' rather than focus on & practice what will make us happy & successful.

@anonymousmethod

The most empowering thing you can do is to tell someone that you believe in them.

@anonymousmethod

Practice kindness before it slips away, like your mother tongue when you don't use it.

@anonymousmethod

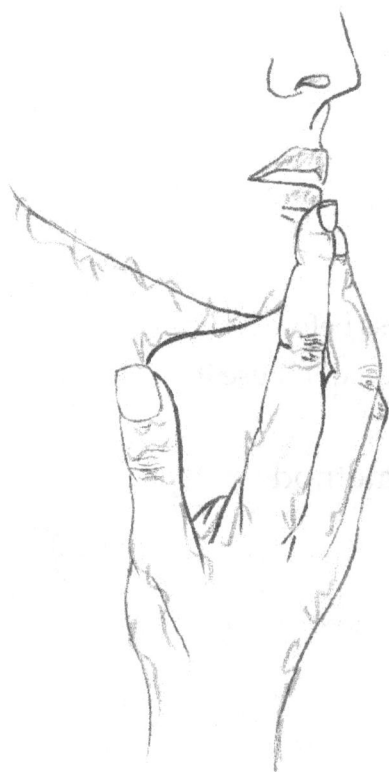

We live in a society where from the fancy clubs, they take cabs back home to the projects & from the dingy, hipster clubs they go home to the nice parts of town.

@anonymousmethod

Talent grows out of curiosity, anger, revenge & dissatisfaction at life, not comfort. The comfortable ones are too content to make the bold moves required to explore & share their talent with the world.

@anonymousmethod

We love the idea of an artist, but not until they've 'made it.'

@anonymousmethod

What you want & need isn't as important as what the world wants & needs. Use your story to heal the world & make it a better place.

@anonymousmethod

Today the barista that made your coffee, the driver that drove you, the shop assistant that helped pack your groceries, were all trying their best not to fall apart. We never know what people are going through and what their smile is hiding. Please treat people with kindness

@anonymousmethod

We talk of behaviours that we won't tolerate so much that we forget to appreciate the virtues of a person that implore us to stay. Remember to look for the green flags too.

@anonymousmethod

If we lose the ability to be vulnerable, we lose the ability to connect.

@anonymousmethod

.

Life spoiler alert; The kind-hearted win in the end.

@anonymousmethod

Breaking generational curses & backward cultural
norms will have people looking at you like you're
crazy. People will dismiss you, talk shit about you and
the worst ones; those that admire you but are too scared
to join you, will leave you for dead.

@anonymousmethod

Tell people you appreciate them. Just drop them a text/call whenever you think of them. It doesn't have to be a full-blown conversation, but just a thought. You never know they may just need that to get them through the day.

@anonymousmethod

A conversation is not a monologue. Listen.

@anonymousmethod

Don't do things half-heartedly. Either do them properly or move on. Don't waste your time living a life that you're not excited about.

@anonymousmethod

Whilst you're feeling down, remember this; some of your best days haven't even taken place yet. There are gonna be parties that will leave you dancing till sunrise, random adventures with people that you haven't even met yet that will get your adrenaline rushing. You're gonna meet someone & you're just gonna click. You will get that life changing phone call. life is going to exceed your expectations. You must stay focused, continue to work hard & keep on saying yes. Remember you haven't felt it all, the universe has so much to give you

@anonymousmethod

Without Stella Adler, we would have no Marlon Brando. Without Elia Kazan, we would have no James Dean. Without Coppola, we would have no Al Pacino. Without Steve Wozniak, we would have no Steve Jobs. Without Sir Alex Ferguson, there would be no Cristiano Ronaldo. When you find talent that you believe in, help them up. Send the elevator back down and invest in them, don't let them waste away.

@anonymousmethod

Find the inner child in yourself. Look closely at the wounds, the trauma, the early battles and the abuse that you endured. Here you will find your truths; as to why you are the way you are. The road to recovery starts here.

@anonymousmethod

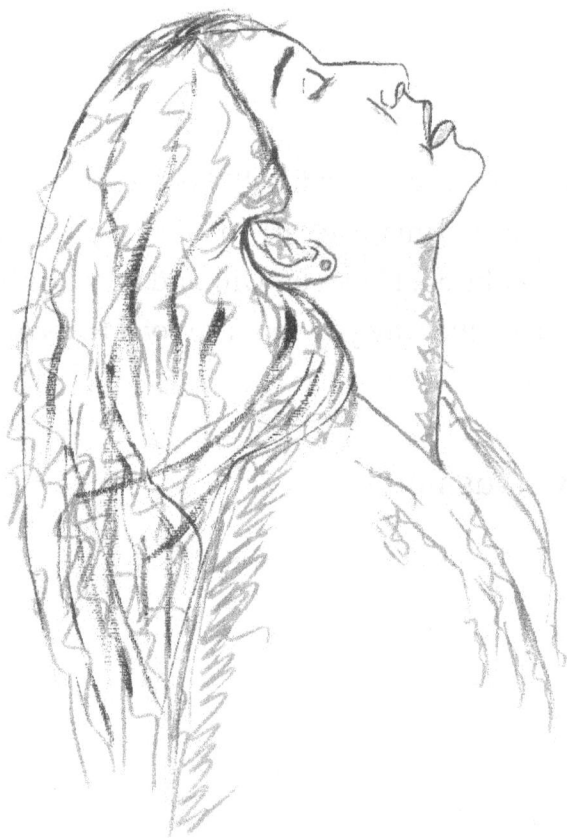

Be the reason someone believes in people again, even if they don't believe in you at first.

@anonymousmethod

I've been to three funerals of people who took their lives. The recurring theme was that these people were described as kind, selfless, happy, funny, hardworking & loving. This told me everything I needed to know about today's society & how we treat people.

@anonymousmethod

Clever people think they're stupid, stupid people think they're clever & idiots think they're geniuses.

@anonymousmethod

People like me don't have people. We are the people that people have.

@anonymousmethod

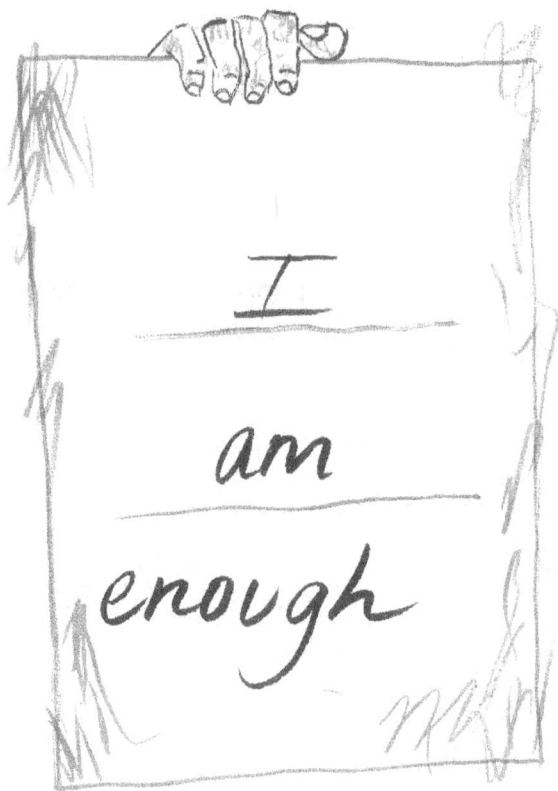

I

am

enough

People always ask me why I'm nice to people, even though they are rude to me? It's because I have been rude to nice people & I know that rudeness comes from a place of pain & only kindness soothes it.

@anonymousmethod

Take this time to get to know your parents. Ask them about their childhood, about the challenges they faced & their parents. Ask them what it was like to raise you and about your life through their eyes. Ask them what makes them tick. Ask them what their favourite colour is, their favourite food growing up, their favourite place and their favourite memory of you together. Really get to know them, for this will bring you closer and you will see the very threads from which the cloth you are cut from is woven. With this, you will find the compassion, empathy and understanding you need to bring it back to how it used to be.

@anonymousmethod

We say we want straight up honest, kind, genuine, caring with no drama, but when they come along, we don't know what to do. We get so freaked out that we push them away. Why? Well it's because your body is so used to a certain level of cortisol, the stress hormone. Since childhood you've been brought up in an environment that induced it. Heal from your childhood and you'll see your world change.

@anonymousmethod

When a person makes you suffer, it's because they're suffering deep down inside & its spilling over. It's a cry for help. Be patient with them. Help them, don't punish them.

@anonymousmethod

Never regret being a caring person. Whoever got to experience your love, probably needed it at the time.

@anonymousmethod

Do not go around hurting people. Leave people better than you found them, even if they've done you wrong. If they hurt you because they didn't trust you, then leave them with a taste of trust and a sense of belief that there are good people out there, just like yourself. Maybe one day they'll come back and thank you for it & even if they don't, at least you can live knowing that you did the right thing. I promise you, one day someone will walk into your life and appreciate how amazing you are.

@anonymousmethod

People hurt you because they're still unhealed from childhood trauma. They didn't get the love they needed growing up. And no one was there to hold their hand & guide them through their rotten childhood. It's heart-breaking to see so much of this in the world today, but what's even more heart-breaking is the fact that they are in denial, so they don't address the issues.

@anonymousmethod

Artistic character is heavily suffused with empathy & kindness.

@anonymousmethod

The most naïve thing we can do is not pay attention to people with a positive attitude. We stupidly think that they're naïve, stupid or uneducated. It's quite the contrary.

@anonymousmethod

All humans are dreamers, but they pretend to be cynics because they are terrified of wanting something they may never get.

@anonymousmethod

I attract people because I am authentic, but soon I scare them away because I also demand the same authenticity from them and of themselves.

@anonymousmethod

I'm not interested in whether you've stood next to successful people. I'm interested in whether you've sat with the broken.

@anonymousmethod

You've been chosen to break generational curses. That's why things don't come easy for you. I know it sucks, but you're the one who your bloodline has been waiting for. Don't give up. You're almost there. Don't give up on the people around you. They need you.

@anonymousmethod

You work so damn hard, you give it your all every single time you do something. You are the kindest, most selfless person I've ever known. I've seen you knock at doors most people are scared to knock. I know no one has let you in yet, but my god, when some does, they are not gonna regret it. I know sometimes it's hard and you can't see the light at the end of the tunnel, but keep at it. You probably quit daily in your mind, but please just hold on for a little longer, your time is about to come.

@anonymousmethod

You start talking to someone, things are going well, almost good enough to get into the 'relationship' phase. Then out of nowhere, they pull back. They start leaving you on read, the energy isn't the same. Well, my theory is 'the better you are, the more likely you are to get curved, because as a good person, you bring out the commitment issues in a person. They start seeing a future with you & they think 'this is too good to be true'. They put on their glasses to take a closer look, but what they don't realise is that their glasses are fogged by their past, which keeps on telling them 'it won't last, just like the last.'

@anonymousmethod

When someone cries because you said something nice to them, you need to protect them because they haven't seen enough kindness in the world.

@anonymousmethod

You're different. You wanna break boundaries & you're brave enough to think you can. You wanna change the world by doing something extraordinary. Your journey won't be an easy one. No one will stand by your side, because you'll seem crazy, but one day everyone will want a piece of your time. Don't let the loneliness that you're going through make you veer off your path. The world needs you.

@anonymousmethod

Acting is not about being famous, it's about exploring the human soul. Fame is just a waste product of acting.

@anonymousmethod

Don't go into the arts thinking that you'll make money. You probably won't. Do it because you enjoy it. Creating art will help you learn, heal and grow as a person. Look at society and create art that will serve it. To better it. That is the point of art... Maybe then you might make a few quid.

@anonymousmethod

Make art with the intention of addressing the whole world. And make sure it's of such high importance, that the whole world will want to listen.

@anonymousmethod

Audiences don't come to see you, they come to see themselves, so show them something that will move them.

@anonymousmethod

And despite the fact that she broke his heart, he spoke
to her with the same respect and love. Years later she
realized that she had taken a major loss in her life. But
by then, it was all too late. He had found someone who
didn't take his love for granted.

@anonymousmethod

Dear minorities & the working class, the arts aren't a place where you just entertain the rich and the majority, where you nourish their preconceptions of us. Yes, this will put food on your table, but I promise you it won't feed your soul. It won't fulfil that desire you went into the arts for in the first place. Art should be a reflection of your reality. Tell your truth, period. Let's stop playing stereotypes and creating caricatures.

@anonymousmethod

Choosing to be an artist isn't your first choice or your second choice, it's your only choice.

@anonymousmethod

Everyone experiences trauma, you can't avoid it nor can you protect your loved ones completely. But what you can do is be there for people when they go through it. Listen to them vent & cry. Help them understand it. This way it'll leave less of a scar.

@anonymousmethod

An honest writer's journey is a slow, painful one.
People will admire you, but from a distance. They will
dismiss you as you go from 'menial job' to 'menial job'.
You've dedicated your entire life to telling stories that
matter. Stories that will change society for the better.
Why? Because you need to get your truth out and you
know the importance of sharing this with the world.
Telling stories makes life more bearable for you. You
have no other option, nor would you want one. So stay
strong, for it will be worth it in the end. Those that
watched you from a distance & never stuck around,
will tell the story of when they once met you.

@anonymousmethod

When you're young everyone tells you to have courage and explore the unexplored path, to reach for the stars. So, you do just that, but then society, including 'your people' leave you hanging. You're left in no man's land with little support. So, most retreat and go back to a miserable, safe life. Whilst the lucky few come out on the other side as successful, but covered in scars.

@anonymousmethod

The kindest people are kind because they grew up in a house that was not kind to them. They've been through so much at the hands of the people that were 'meant' to love them the most, but they refuse to let these experiences turn them cynical, bitter and grow a hard shell. They know the only way forward is to be kind, empathetic, caring and to love again, because they never would want anyone to go through the pain that they've been through. If that isn't something to be in awe of, then I really don't know what is.

@anonymousmethod

Sometimes God sends you an angel. They're guided by unconditional love. No matter where you are in life, no matter how many battle scars you have, what your past was like, they still believe in you. They see through everything. They see you for what you are truly worth and that you have a greater purpose in life. They will believe in you & push you to do great things. If you come across these people, hold them tight. And if you don't come across them, become one of them.

@anonymousmethod

You looked lovingly into my eyes but through glasses that were fogged by your past. So, you never got to see the real me. Now I'm left with just memories. I guess I'll just turn my pain into art & maybe through that you'll get to know the real me.

@anonymousmethod

The best art comes from those who feel like they don't belong' for art is a way of proving your existence.

@anonymousmethod

I don't get it when people say, "Don't cross oceans for people who wouldn't cross a puddle for you". No, I think you should. Help everyone. Be kind. Love again, unconditionally this time. Don't worry about whether they'll reciprocate or not. Just focus on being a good person. In life and love, it isn't about what you gain, it's about what you give.

@anonymousmethod

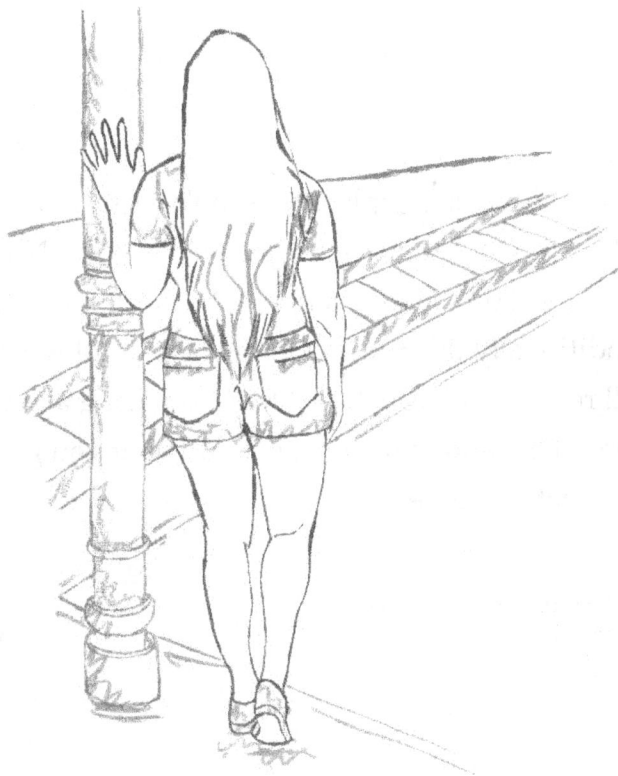

We are all living with the fear of missing out on something better, all the while overlooking the beauty of what we have right in front of us. This will lead to us becoming old and regretful.

@anonymousmethod

The best art comes from those who feel like they don't belong, for art is a way of proving your existence.

@anonymousmethod

Minorities can't tell the truth, unless it comes with a punchline.

@anonymousmethod

When someone who has been sad, distant and not themselves for a while, suddenly starts going out of their way to see people, often giving gifts or possessions, don't assume they 'got better'. This is the time to really ask them if they're ok' reach out and not simply accept the answer of "I'm fine" or "great". Because for some people the relief of having made the decision of ending their life can make them happy, euphoric even. The change in behaviour is their way of them saying goodbye.

@anonymousmethod

The problem with today's society is that we don't take the time to get to know and understand one another. We just make assumptions with our poor attitude. So, we dispose of people just like that, which leaves them broken.

@anonymousmethod

Patience is when you heart burns but you remain silent.

@anonymousmethod

You cannot raise your children the way your parents raised you because the world that they raised you in no longer exists. Lets adapt before we destroy yet another generation.

@anonymousmethod

Did I actually write all of this or am I just subconsciously plagurising things ive heard in the past?

@anonymousmethod

www.ingramcontent.com/pod-product-compliance
Lightning Source LLC
Chambersburg PA
CBHW060015050426
42448CB00012B/2758